SPORTS MVPs

GIANNIS ANTETOKOUNMPO

BY JAGGER YOUSSEF

Gareth Stevens
PUBLISHING

Please visit our website, www.garethstevens.com. For a free color catalog of all our high-quality books, call toll free 1-800-542-2595 or fax 1-877-542-2596.

Library of Congress Cataloging-in-Publication Data

Names: Youssef, Jagger, author.
Title: Giannis Antetokounmpo / Jagger Youssef.
Description: New York : Gareth Stevens Publishing, [2024] | Series: Sports MVPs | Includes bibliographical references and index.
Identifiers: LCCN 2023013166 (print) | LCCN 2023013167 (ebook) | ISBN 9781538285909 (library binding) | ISBN 9781538285893 (paperback) | ISBN 9781538285916 (ebook)
Subjects: LCSH: Antetokounmpo, Giannis, 1994—Biography–Juvenile literature. | Basketball players–Greece–Biography–Juvenile literature. | Milwaukee Bucks (Basketball team)–History–Juvenile literature. | National Basketball Association–Juvenile literature.
Classification: LCC GV884.A56 Y6 2024 (print) | LCC GV884.A56 (ebook) | DDC 796.323092 [B]–dc23/eng/20230413
LC record available at https://lccn.loc.gov/2023013166
LC ebook record available at https://lccn.loc.gov/2023013167

Published in 2024 by
Gareth Stevens Publishing
2544 Clinton St,
Buffalo, NY 14224

Designer: Claire Wrazin
Editor: Therese Shea

Photo credits: Cover, pp. 1, 9 Ververidis Vasilis/Shutterstock.com; pp. 5, 15, 17, 19 Erik Drost/flickr; p. 7 sixtwelve/flickr; p. 11 Cal Sport Media/Alamy Stock Photo; p. 13 UPI/Alamy Stock Photo; p. 21 All-Pro Reels/flickr.

Printed in the United States of America

CPSIA compliance information: Batch #CS24GS: For further information contact Gareth Stevens, New York, New York at 1-800-542-2595.

CONTENTS

A Name to Remember. 4
Discovered in Greece 6
On to the NBA 10
Becoming an All-Star 12
NBA MVP 16
NBA Champion 18
Record Breaker 20
Glossary. 22
For More Information. 23
Index 24

Boldface words appear in the glossary.

A Name to Remember

Giannis Antetokounmpo is a star **forward** in the NBA (National Basketball Association). This is how you say his name: YAHN-iss ah-deh-toh-KOON-boh. Giannis was born December 6, 1994, in Athens, Greece. His parents were from Nigeria. They moved to Europe for a better life.

Hotels.com
ALL-STAR
NBA
StateFarm
R 2022

Discovered in Greece

But life was hard at first in Greece. Giannis's family did not have Greek **citizenship**. It was not easy for them to find jobs. Giannis and his brothers sold things on the streets to make money for their family.

THANASIS AND GIANNIS ANTETOKOUNMPO
IN SEPOLIA, GREECE

When Giannis was 13, a basketball coach spotted him playing tag. The coach asked Giannis and his brothers to play for his basketball club. He found Giannis's parents jobs too. Three years later, Giannis was playing **semipro** basketball.

34

On to the NBA

Giannis's skills were noticed in the United States. When he turned 18, he entered the 2013 NBA **draft**. He was picked 15th overall by the Milwaukee Bucks. He became one of the youngest NBA players ever. Giannis made the NBA All-**Rookie** Team.

BUCKS
34

Becoming an All-Star

Giannis worked on his skills his first few years in the NBA. In 2016, he became the youngest Milwaukee Buck to record a **triple-double**. In 2017, he led the Bucks in points, **rebounds**, steals, **assists**, and blocks!